HEINEMANN STATE STUDIES

People of
California

Mir Tamim Ansary

Heinemann Library
Chicago, Illinois

Designed by Heinemann Library
Page layout by Depke Design
Printed and bound in the United States by
 Lake Book Manufacturing, Inc.

07 06 05 04 03
10 9 8 7 6 5 4 3 2 1

**Library of Congress
Cataloging-in-Publication Data**

Ansary, Mir Tamim.
People of California / by Mir Tamim Ansary.
p. cm. -- (Heinemann state studies)
Summary: Examines the diversity of peoples
who inhabit California, including ethnic groups
and immigrants, and profiles such successful
Californians as Kareem Abdul Jabbar, Shirley
Temple, and Ralph Bunche.

Includes bibliographical references (p.) and index.

ISBN 1-40340-342-2 -- ISBN 1-40340-559-X (pbk.)
1. California--Ethnic relations--Juvenile literature.
2. Ethnology--California--Juvenile literature. 3.
Minorities--California--Juvenile literature. 4. Immi-
grants--California--Juvenile literature. 5. California-
-Population--Juvenile literature. 6. California--Biog-
raphy--Juvenile literature. 7. Successful people--
California--Biography--Juvenile literature. [1. Cal-
ifornia--Population. 2. Ethnology--California. 3.
Minorities--California. 4. Immigrants--California.
5. California--Biography.] I. Title. II. Series.
F870.A1A57 2002
305.8'009794--dc21

2002010883

Acknowledgments
The author and publishers are grateful to the
following for permission to reproduce copyright
material:

Cover photographs by (top, L-R) AP Wide World
Photo, The Granger Collection, National Archives,
Brown Brothers, (main) Lawrence Migdale

Title page (L-R) Mark L. Stephenson/Corbis,
Lawrence Migdale, AP Wide World Photo; contents
page (L-R) Hulton-Deutsch Collection/Corbis,
The Granger Collection, Andy Kuno/AP Wide
World Photo; pp. 4, 27 Nik Wheeler; pp. 7, 19, 23,
25 Lawrence Migdale; p. 8 David Turnley/Corbis;
pp. 9, 16, 35T, 36T, 42 Brown Brothers; pp. 11,
31B Roger Ressmeyer/Corbis; p. 12 Jan Butchofsky-
Houser/Corbis; p. 13 Robert Holmes; p. 15T Chuck
Pefley; pp. 15B, 28, 29 Bettmann/Corbis; p. 17
Robert Holmes/Corbis; p. 18T Ted Streshinsky/
Corbis; pp. 18B, 24, 33, 38, 43B The Granger
Collection; pp. 20T, 35B Hulton-Deutsch
Collection/Corbis; p. 20B Rich Pedroncelli/AP Wide
World Photo; pp. 21, 44 AFP/Corbis; p. 22 Steve
Jay Crise/Corbis; p. 26 Mark L. Stephenson/Corbis;
p. 30T Andy Kuno/AP Wide World Photo; pp. 30B,
37T, 39T, 40, 41B, 43T AP Wide World Photo;
p. 31T Rob Schumacher/AP Wide World Photo;
p. 32 Huntington Library; pp. 34, 39B, 41T Corbis;
p. 36B Lois Bernstein/AP Wide World Photo; p. 37B
Phoebe Hearst Museum of Anthropology/
University of California at Berkeley; p. 45
maps.com/Heinemann Library

Photo research by Julie Laffin

Thanks to expert reader, author, and editor,
Marlene Smith-Baranzini, M.A., for her help in the
preparation of this book. Also, special thanks to
Lucinda Surber for her curriculum guidance.

Every effort has been made to contact copyright
holders of any material reproduced in this book.
Any omissions will be rectified in subsequent
printings if notice is given to the publisher.

Some words are shown in bold, **like this.**
You can find out what they mean by looking
in the glossary.

Contents

California: A Diverse State

Picture yourself on a bus in Los Angeles or San Francisco. Look around, and you will see people from many different backgrounds. Listen, and you will hear many accents and some foreign languages. At least five million Californians speak Spanish, and three million others speak Chinese, Tagalog, Vietnamese, Hindi, Farsi, or Japanese.

California's many large cities include Los Angeles, the second biggest city in the United States.

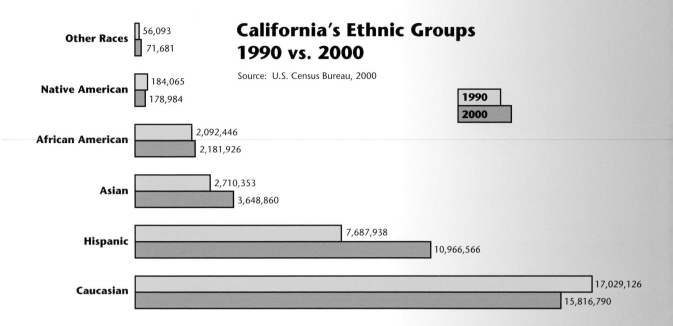

California's Ethnic Groups 1990 vs. 2000

Source: U.S. Census Bureau, 2000

| | 1990 | 2000 |

Other Races: 56,093 / 71,681

Native American: 184,065 / 178,984

African American: 2,092,446 / 2,181,926

Asian: 2,710,353 / 3,648,860

Hispanic: 7,687,938 / 10,966,566

Caucasian: 17,029,126 / 15,816,790

ETHNIC GROUPS

California is home to many **minority** groups. In California, even the largest **ethnic** group, people of European background, add up to less than one half of the total population. About one-third of the people in California are **Latino.** Their roots go back to a Spanish-speaking country in North, Central, or South America. Many California Latinos speak English as their first language, but their parents or grandparents grew up speaking Spanish.

Almost one-fifth of Californians have roots going back to various parts of Asia. They or their ancestors came from China, Japan, Vietnam, Cambodia, Laos, or Korea. Orange County is home to the largest Vietnamese community outside of Vietnam. The largest community of Afghans outside of Asia is the estimated 40,000 who live in the San Francisco Bay Area. Similar claims can be made for Koreans, Asian Indians, and many other ethnic groups.

Between 1990 and 2000, the Hispanic and Asian populations rose while the number of Caucasians in California fell.

About one out of every twenty Californians is African American. This means their **ancestry** can be traced back to some part of the continent of Africa. Los Angeles has more Mexicans than any city in Mexico except for Mexico City. Other Californians have come from India, Armenia, Turkey, the Pacific Islands, and other places, though their numbers in California are much smaller.

The history of California Native Americans is a different story from that of other **ethnic** groups who **immigrated** to the state. Native Americans have lived in the area for more than 10,000 years. Today, California has more Native Americans than any other state except Oklahoma. Not all of

All of California's ten largest cities increased in population between the years 1990 and 2000.

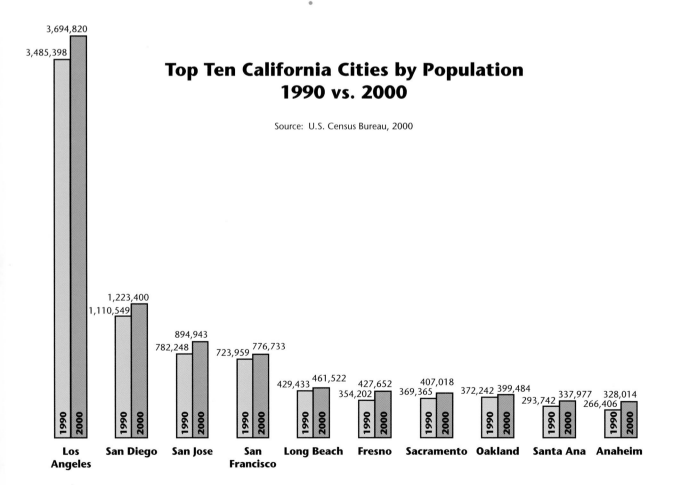

Top Ten California Cities by Population 1990 vs. 2000

Source: U.S. Census Bureau, 2000

them have ancient roots in this state. Very few, in fact, **descended** from California's original people. Many moved to California from other states when the U.S. government was **relocating** groups of Native American people.

From gold rush days, people from around the country and the world have viewed California as a land of opportunity. Today, the faces of its people reflect every area of the globe, as new arrivals come to claim their "California dream." Each group of people brings different traditions, values, cultural beliefs, and ideas to California. Together, these groups have helped California achieve great things. California is often the world leader in new inventions, technologies, and entertainment, thanks to the **diversity** of its people.

Native Languages

Native Americans of California spoke over 100 different languages before Europeans arrived. Today, however, most Native American children grow up speaking English. As a result, at least 50 Native American languages in California are in danger of dying out. California has the greatest number of endangered languages in North America.

*People from many lands and many **cultures** have settled in California.*

Population Movements

Every ten years, the U.S. government counts the nation's people. This count is called the **census.** The census also finds out how many people are male, how many are female, how many belong to each **ethnic** group, and other such information.

During the 1970s and 1980s, census data showed that California had grown twice as fast as the average growth of all the other states. In the 1990s, growth slowed. For two years, California's growth even dropped below the national average. During those years, many people moved out of California because prices were high, and there were few jobs. But others were still coming to California, especially from other countries, so the population kept rising.

RUSHING TO CALIFORNIA (1500–1900s)

Throughout history, California has seen waves of newcomers. The first were **immigrants** from Mexico. They moved to California from the 1500s through the 1830s. The next big wave of immigrants came during the gold rush, which

This Mexican woman and her children are waiting to cross the border into California, where she hopes to find work.

began in 1848. People came because they heard they could get rich mining gold or find other jobs in California. The state's population tripled in three years. Two of California's major cities, San Francisco and Sacramento, were born at that time. After the gold rush died down in the 1850s, people kept trickling in, hoping to get rich from silver and other opportunities.

In 1870, there was another rush. This time people poured into southern California. They heard about life being pleasant, easy, and healthful in that part of California. Some have called this the "land rush," because many people got rich selling land to the newcomers.

Then, in 1892, oil was discovered in Los Angeles, setting off an "oil rush." At the same time, a "film rush" began. Young people came to Los Angeles hoping to get into movies. The balance of the state's population shifted from the north, where the mining was, to the south, and it has never shifted back.

LOOKING FOR AN EASIER LIFE (1930–PRESENT)

In the 1930s, many people came to California from Oklahoma and Arkansas. Drought caused their crops to

Many groups suffered terrible hardships on the difficult trail to California during the gold rush.

fail, and with no income, they lost their land. They believed stories they heard about easy living in California. The population of the Central Valley, where the land was good for farming, grew dramatically for the first time.

During and after World War II (1939–1945), people came to the coastal cities to work in factories that made airplanes and other products for war. Many of these people were African Americans from the southeastern United States. **Immigration** from Mexico rose in these years as well.

The entertainment business—especially the music **industry**—was soaring during the 1960s. Surf music became popular when a group called the Beach Boys began performing songs like "Surfin' USA." San Francisco's Haight-Ashbury district was home to "hippies" and "flower children." Acid rock became popular as well, played by California-based groups such as the Grateful Dead and Jefferson Airplane. In 1962, California became the state in the nation with the largest population, jumping from 9 million residents around 1940 to 22 million people.

California's Immigration Station

In 1910, the "Ellis Island of the West," Angel Island, opened in China Cove. However, immigrants from China, Japan, and other Asian countries soon realized upon arrival that acts and laws passed against them would play major roles in their American lives. Between 1910 and 1940, as many as 175,000 Chinese and 60,000 Japanese immigrants endured crowded facilities, scary medical examinations, intense questioning, and countless days of waiting at the Angel Island Immigration Station.

During the 1970s and 1980s, large numbers of **refugees** came to California from **war-torn** lands in Asia, Central America, and Africa. People coming by ship landed here because it was the first state they reached, and it had the biggest ports. Refugees and **immigrants** found it easy to fit into the **diverse** population of California.

One-quarter of the people living in California today were born in another country. Many others came from other U.S. states. People move around within California as well. It is not uncommon for someone born in the state to move to another part of California later in life.

Refugees from Laos, in Southeast Asia, came to California in the 1980s to escape the war zone their homeland had become.

In the 1980s and 1990s, the computer industry bloomed in northern California. People came to the area to get jobs and to take part in an exciting age of invention and creativity. Over 2.3 million people now live in the Silicon Valley area.

Recently, more immigrants have been settling in the Central Valley, away from the coast. Many are moving to the **foothills** of the Sierra Nevada. One reason for this is that land and houses have become more expensive along the coast, especially in major cities. The cost of living is lower in the **inland** counties, the fastest-growing regions in California today.

Cultural Groups in California

Culture in California is a mixture of many flavors, because the people living here have come from so many places. Each group has contributed something to the art and style of the state.

Native Americans were living in California when the first groups of Europeans arrived. European Americans form the largest group in California, but they are not really a single group. Europe is a continent of many cultures. The first Europeans to colonize this land came from Spain in the 1600s. Their **legacy** is reflected in many California place names. *Los Angeles,* for example, means "The Angels" in Spanish. The word *San* is Spanish for "saint." Any city that begins with *San* or *Santa* is named for a Spanish saint.

Mission *San Francisco Solano was built in the Spanish style that is now common in California.*

SPANISH MISSIONARIES

San Francisco was named for a **monk** from the Middle Ages named Saint Francis. He started an **order** of traveling religious people called **friars.** Franciscan friars built religious communities called **missions** in California. They were hoping to convert the Native Americans to **Christianity.** They started California's first cattle ranches and wineries. The first towns developed around missions.

The Franciscan friars left their mark in the "Spanish-style" house that can be seen across California. These houses are made of **adobe** coated with stucco, which is a rough plaster made of cement, sand, and limestone. These houses are often whitewashed, or made to look white. The roofs are covered with orange rounded clay tiles. There are many houses like this in southern California. San Francisco and San Jose have whole neighborhoods of them, too.

As the gold rush began, English-speaking newcomers traveling from the eastern United States overpowered the Spanish influence. These people spoke the English language, but few had English roots. Instead, many had a mixed Northern

The Spanish Franciscan fathers laid the foundation for California's wine industry in 1823 when Padre Jose Altimera planted several thousand grapevines at San Francisco Solano in Sonoma.

The English in California

English **immigrants** did not settle in California in big numbers. One well-known explorer who did come was Sir Francis Drake. He was a ship captain who stopped near San Francisco Bay in 1579, on a trip around the world. Another famous English visitor to California was author Robert Louis Stevenson. He lived in California from 1879 to 1881, and again in 1888. It was here that he got the idea for his famous novel *Treasure Island*, an adventure story about pirates. Other English immigrants came to California and chose to stay.

European background. Those who stayed after the gold rush built wooden frame houses like they were used to in places like New England.

ITALIAN AMERICANS

Some gold rush **immigrants** came directly from foreign countries, such as Italy. Most of the Italian immigrants quickly gave up mining for farming. They discovered how rich the soil was in California's valleys, especially those in the Coast Range, such as Napa and Sonoma. The land and climate is similar to Italy. Italians found they could successfully grow crops they were used to, such as nuts, olives, and grapes.

When word of their good life got back to Italy, their relatives and friends came over, too. **Immigration** from Italy was at its highest during the 1880s. By 1940, Italians made up the largest European community in California.

Early Italian immigrants settled in a neighborhood called North Beach on San Francisco Bay. As San Francisco expanded, it absorbed the small community. North Beach became what it is today: the city's "Italian"

Coffeehouses and other restaurants owned by Italian immigrants are found in many Italian districts of California cities.

neighborhood, loaded with Italian restaurants, coffeehouses, and **delicatessens.**

The Italian **legacy** can also be seen in the California wine **industry.** Italian families founded the popular Gallo, C. K. Mondavi, Sebastiani, Franzia, Coppolas, and Italian Swiss Colony wineries.

Amadeo Giannini founded the Bank of America.

In 1904, Amadeo P. Giannini founded the Bank of Italy to serve "the little people." After the San Francisco earthquake of 1906, he set up a table on the docks and loaned money requiring only "a face and a signature." His company, which became the Bank of America, created many banking practices used today. By 1945, it had grown into the world's largest bank.

San Francisco Stew

One contribution Italian immigrants made to California **culture** is *ciopinno*, a rich fish stew flavored with tomato sauce. *Ciopinno* was not brought from Italy, but was invented in San Francisco's Italian community. The coffeehouse was another Italian contribution.

IRISH AMERICANS

The first Irish **immigrants** came to California in the Spanish era, before the 1840s, but the flow picked up during the gold rush. They came not just to find gold, but also to escape hunger. Ireland was going through a potato **famine** from 1845 through 1850. The poor people of Ireland lived almost entirely on potatoes, and a disease wiped out the whole crop.

An Irishman named James Phelan served as mayor of San Francisco from 1897 to 1901, and then as a U.S. senator from 1915 to 1921.

Irish **immigration** peaked in the 1870s, after the U.S. Civil War, when the United States Congress passed legislation (1864–1868) encouraging people to come and help settle the land in the West. Many immigrants who came to California helped build the **transcontinental** railroad. Most of the Irish went to work as factory workers or on the docks, loading ships. Some found success in politics. John Downey, for example, became California's seventh governor in 1860. Other Irishmen, such as John Mackay, James Flood, and William S. O'Brien, built their fortunes in silver mining.

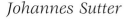

Johannes Sutter

GERMAN AMERICANS

The history of famous Germans in California begins with a German-born Swiss named Johannes Sutter. The gold that started the gold rush was found on his land. But instead of getting rich, Sutter lost everything he owned to **squatters** who mined and settled on his land illegally.

Other German immigrants had better success. Charles Krug and the Wente Brothers started wine companies. Charles Spreckels made his fortune in sugar, earning the title of "The Sugar King." German-born movie artists, such as actress Marlene Dietrich, were successful in Hollywood.

Many Jewish-German immigrants went into the grocery or clothing businesses. Levi Strauss founded the company that invented blue jeans. A few, such as Adolph Sutro, went into banking. Others of Jewish **ancestry** helped found the movie **industry.**

The Spreckels Mansion, the San Diego home of Charles Spreckels, is now a hotel.

FRENCH AMERICANS

About 4,000 French men and women trickled into California after the gold rush. Some made money running department stores. Others made money as sheep ranchers. One Frenchman, Paul Masson, started a highly successful winery.

ARMENIAN AMERICANS

The Central Valley has one of the largest Armenian populations in the United States. Between the 1880s and

This image, taken in 1977, shows an Armenian-American couple standing in their vineyard in Fresno, California.

the 1920s, the Armenians were terrorized by the Turks, and over a million of them were killed. Many of the survivors escaped to the United States. Those who came to California settled in and around the city of Fresno in the Central Valley. They were drawn to this area because the climate and the soil reminded them of home. They grew crops such as figs, nuts, raisins, and melons.

Famous Armenians of California include writer William Saroyan, who won the **Pulitzer Prize** in 1939. George Deukmejian, another **descendant** of Armenian **immigrants** to the state, was governor of California from 1983 to 1991.

William Saroyan at age 27

LATINO AMERICANS

Latinos form the second largest **ethnic** group in California, after Europeans. Along with Asians, the Latino population is growing at ten times the rate of other ethnic groups. Although they have a Spanish-speaking background, few are descended from the original Spanish colonists. For the most part, their roots go back to Mexico, Central America, and South America. Many came to California in the 1900s.

Immigration from Mexico increased rapidly during World War II. At that time, many workers were moving from

farms to cities to take jobs in the factories. This left the farms short of labor. The richest farmers appealed to the U.S. government for help. The government then made an

Migrant farm workers did hard work for low pay until they formed a union called the United Farm Workers.

agreement with Mexico, and the two countries set up the *bracero* program. Mexican citizens could now come to the United States to work on farms during a growing season and then return home. These traveling workers became known as **migrant farm workers.**

Hundreds of thousands of Mexicans took advantage of the offer. Many stayed in California and became U.S. citizens. In fact, the jobs in the north tempted many to come in without papers or permission.

The migrant workers lived a hard life. They had to move from field to field to find work. They slept in camps set up by the growers. They could never be sure if they would have jobs from one month to the next. They earned and owned little. A man named César Chávez decided to do something about this. In 1962, he organized a **union,** later called the United Farm

César Chávez fought for rights of farm workers.

Workers (UFW). When grape pickers went on **strike,** the UFW supported them. They urged other farm workers to **strike,** too.

But Chávez went one step further. He asked the public to support the strike with a **boycott.** The UFW called a boycott on table grapes and later on lettuce. This new nonviolent **tactic** put pressure on growers because it cost them money when people did not buy the products. Chávez also **fasted** publicly to call attention to the problems of the farm workers. In the 1970s, the UFW finally won the right to represent farm workers.

Also in the 1970s, **immigration** from the south rose again. This time, however, many **immigrants** were coming from other countries in Central and South America, as well as Mexico. Those people were running from terrible wars raging in their homelands. Some became **migrant farm workers,** too.

Migrant farm workers move often from one farm to the next. They work long hours in the hot sun, picking the crops for landowners.

Latino Culture

Of course, **Latino culture** in California is not limited to farm workers. More people of Mexican **descent** live in Los Angeles than in any other city, except Mexico City, Mexico. Business ownership in Los Angeles is rising faster among Latinos than any other group.

Several people of Latino descent have played a role in California politics. Cruz Bustamente was elected **lieutenant governor** in the year 2000. Ron Gonzales became mayor of San Jose in 1998. Loretta Sanchez was elected for her third term in the U.S. Congress in 2000.

Playwright Luis Valdez founded Teatro Campesino as part of the farm workers movement. It became an artistic force in American theater. Latino musicians, such as Carlos Santana and Tito Puentes, have influenced jazz, salsa, and rock music. Director Robert Rodriguez has become famous with movies such as *Spy Kids,* which starred California Latino actor Antonio Banderas. Gary Soto of Fresno is an award-winning author of stories, plays, and novels.

Carlos Santana has played his guitar in countless concerts around the world. He is shown here at a concert in Germany in 2000.

The influence of Latino culture is clear everywhere in California. Every big city has excellent Mexican restaurants. Mexicans have deeply influenced the look of California, too. Mexican tilework decorates many buildings. In the larger cities, you often see murals, which are big pictures painted on walls.

Ghost of the Barrio *is typical of the many murals or wall paintings found in Latino neighborhoods in Los Angeles.*

These murals reflect an art style that developed in Mexico and has flourished in California. Often, they offer a collection of images that tell the history of a people or place. Los Angeles is famous for the murals in the *barrio*, its largest **Latino** neighborhood. San Francisco, too, has dozens of murals in the **Mission** District, the main Latino neighborhood of that city.

LATINO CELEBRATIONS

Non-Latinos come out for the colorful parades, fairs, and street dances that are part of Latino celebrations. One of Mexico's most important holidays is Cinco de Mayo, which means "the Fifth of May." On this day in 1867,

Mexico drove out French invaders. It is like a second Mexican Independence Day. Large Cinco de Mayo celebrations take place in the cities of California.

Most California Latinos belong to the **Catholic Church,** so another important festival in this community is Carnival. This is very similar to the French festival in New Orleans, Louisiana, known as Mardi Gras. It falls on the last day before the month of Lent—a time in the spring when **Catholics** traditionally **fast** before Easter.

CHINESE AMERICANS

Asians are the fastest growing group in California, increasing ten times faster than the population of other groups. Chinese Americans form the largest Asian community in the state. They started coming to California in the 1840s. At that time, a **depression** had hit China, and families were sending their sons to California to earn money. These young men often ended up working like slaves for the employers who had brought them over.

The gold rush brought a fresh wave of **immigrants.** By 1852, there were 25,000 Chinese in California. Few searched for gold. Instead, they ran much-needed laundry services and worked in factories. Many Chinese came over

Chinese workers led hard lives in California's gold rush camps. Their clothing and hairstyles made them easy targets for angry American miners.

in the 1860s to work on the **transcontinental** railroad. When the railroad was completed in 1869, workers transferred to various factories, construction companies, fisheries, and canneries. About half the factory workers in San Francisco then were Chinese.

The Chinese often suffered from **discrimination** during the gold rush. Many people were **prejudiced** against them because of their looks and different **customs.** The U.S. government even passed laws that prevented any more people from China from entering the United States. The 1882 Chinese Exclusion Act was one of those laws. Not until 1965 were the last of the laws changed. Only then could Chinese people come here in numbers equal to other groups.

Even after the **immigration** law was banned, the Chinese mostly lived in separate neighborhoods. Since they did not mix with other groups very much, they kept their **culture** alive. One large neighborhood in San Francisco is known as Chinatown. Los Angeles, Sacramento, and Stockton have large Chinatowns, too.

Today, Chinese Californians live in many neighborhoods, but they still look to Chinatowns for a connection to their cultural heritage. Chinatown grocery stores sell specialized items for Chinese cooking. Other stores carry herbs used by Chinese doctors. Some of the best Chinese restaurants in the United States are in California's Chinatowns.

Grant Street is the main street through Chinatown, San Francisco's famous old Chinese neighborhood.

The Lion Dance is often part of Chinese New Year celebrations.

The Chinese celebrate New Year with a big festival in early spring. They observe a twelve-year cycle, with a different animal, such as a dragon, rat, or goat, assigned to each year. During Chinese New Year, people parade through the streets in fancy costumes, carrying huge models of animal symbols and setting off firecrackers.

Chinese Americans have influenced many aspects of California life. In 1990, Chang-Lin Tien became chancellor, or head, of the University of California at Berkeley. March Fong-Eu was California's secretary of state from 1974 to 1994. Writers Amy Tan and Maxine Hong Kingston are both Chinese Americans from California. Wayne Wang is an important film director.

JAPANESE AMERICANS

Japan would not let its own citizens leave the country until 1866. One by one, young single men crossed the Pacific Ocean to California. At first, they worked as gardeners and servants. Over time, they built small businesses, and some were even able to own land.

Trouble for Japanese Americans came in 1942. Japan bombed the U.S. naval base at Pearl Harbor in Hawaii on December 7, 1941. This brought the United States into World War II (1939–1945). Some government officials thought Japanese Americans could not be trusted while the country was at war with Japan. The U.S. government ordered that Japanese Americans be taken to holding camps called internment camps. After the war, the people were released, but most had lost their possessions. Most of the Japanese American population then moved to the Los Angeles area.

Today, Americans agree that it was a mistake for the United States government to question the **loyalty** of its Japanese-American citizens. Not one Japanese American was ever proven guilty of spying. In fact, the 442nd Regimental Combat Team, made up entirely of Japanese Americans, won more medals for bravery than any combat team in U.S. history.

Some Japanese Americans have opened restaurants that feature authentic Japanese foods like sushi and tempura.

Southeast Asians

Other Asian people in California include those from Vietnam and Cambodia, many of whom came here after terrible wars in their homelands. Many **immigrants** from Thailand, the Philippines, Indonesia, and Korea have also come to California.

Prominent Californians of Japanese background include the philosopher S. I. Hayakawa and artist Ruth Asawa. Conductor Seiji Ozawa and cello player Yo Yo Ma are also Japanese Americans.

AFRICAN AMERICANS

When the first Spanish ships arrived in California, their crews included men of African background. Some were slaves, but others were free. They played important roles in colonial life. Francisco Reyes, a Mexican of African **ancestry,** served as mayor of Los Angeles in 1794. Pío Pico, the last Mexican governor of California, was also of African **descent.**

James Beckwourth was a famous scout.

The first American scouts who guided settlers into California included James Beckwourth, an African American. Biddy Mason was a slave who gained her freedom when her master brought her to California during the gold rush era. About 2,000 African Americans lived in California at that time, mostly in the San Francisco area.

In early California, African Americans could not buy land, even if they had the money. It was against the law. They could not testify against a white person in court. They went to separate public schools or none at all, because there was **prejudice** against them.

In the 1900s, California's African-American population grew. About 40,000 African Americans lived in California in the 1920s. Then came World War II (1939–1945), which created thousands of jobs. African Americans moved from the midwest and southeast to work in shipyards, steelmills, and aircraft factories. By 1950, the African-American population in California stood at around 500,000 people—more than four percent of the state's total population.

After the war, opportunities for African Americans decreased. When businesses went through a bad economic cycle, African Americans were often the first to lose their jobs. Anger built up, and in 1965, it led to a **riot** in the Los Angeles neighborhood of Watts. In Oakland, a political group called the Black Panthers formed to address this frustration. Black Panther leaders Bobby Seale, Eldridge Cleaver, and Huey Newton believed the African-American community had to rely on itself.

African Americans have made many gains in California and around the nation. African Americans play leading

The Black Panthers were created to patrol black neighborhoods and protect people from police brutality. After losing the support of black leaders, they shifted their focus to providing social services in black neighborhoods.

A Powerful Politician

African American Willie Brown is one of the most powerful politicians in recent California history. He was elected to the California Assembly seventeen times. As speaker of the assembly, he had  power second only to the governor. After his days in the assembly, Brown became San Francisco's first African-American mayor.

roles in many areas, including California politics. Ronald Dellums of Berkeley was elected to the U.S. Congress in 1970 and served for 27 years. Tom Bradley was a two-term mayor of Los Angeles, first elected in 1973. Wilson Riles ran the state school system as superintendent of education, starting in 1971.

Thomas Bradley

Famous African Americans from California also include Ralph Bunche, who won the **Nobel Peace Prize** in 1950. Working for the United Nations, he helped develop the first peace agreement between Israel and its Arab neighbors. Jackie Robinson, one of baseball's greatest players, grew up in Pasadena, California. Robinson was the first African American to play in the major leagues.

California Achievers

Abdul-Jabbar played for the Los Angeles Lakers from 1975 to 1989.

Abdul-Jabbar, Kareem (b. 1947) Basketball player. Born Lew Alcindor, Jabbar led UCLA to four national championships. He changed his name to Kareem Abdul-Jabbar upon converting to **Islam.** Abdul-Jabbar helped the Los Angeles Lakers win five NBA Championships.

Adams, Ansel (1902–1984) Photographer. Adams started taking pictures of Yosemite Valley with a box camera at age sixteen. He became one of the greatest nature photographers in the United States, turning photography into art.

Alvarado, Juan Bautista (1800–1882) Political leader. A Monterey shipping clerk in 1836, Alvarado led a **revolt** that drove out the governor sent by Mexico City to rule the area. Alvarado ruled California as an independent nation for a few years, but he governed it poorly. Mexico took over again.

Photographer Ansel Adams

Beckwourth, James (1798–1864) Explorer. A skilled Western scout and mountain man, Beckwourth blazed his own trail to California. He discovered what is now Beckwourth Pass and spent ten years guiding settlers and gold miners over the Sierra Nevada Mountains.

Bidwell, John (1819–1900) Rancher, activist. Bidwell proved the value of the Central Valley by turning his 26,000-acre ranch at Chico into a successful wheat farm. Bidwell opposed the U.S. war with Mexico and the mistreatment of the Chinese, among other things.

John Bidwell

Bradley, Thomas (b. 1917) Politician. When he was in college, Bradley moved from Texas to California. Later, he joined the Los Angeles police department and became the city's first African-American police chief. After earning a law degree, he became Los Angeles's first African-American mayor.

Brannan, Samuel (1819–1899) Publisher, **entrepreneur.** Brannan published California's first newspaper, and he broke the news that gold had been discovered at Sutter's Mill. During the gold rush, he became San Francisco's first millionaire. He lived like a king and developed the Calistoga Hot Springs resort.

Samuel Brannan

Bridges, Harry (1901–1990) Labor leader. In 1934, as head of the International Longshore Workers **Union,** Bridges led a successful 83-day **strike** that eventually shut down San Francisco ports for three days. Bridges was tried for **treason** in the 1950s, but was found not guilty. In 1975, San Francisco held a party to honor Bridges as one of its most important citizens.

Brown, Edmund G. "Jerry" Jr. (b. 1938) Politician. Brown entered politics after studying to be a priest. The son of a governor, Brown was himself elected governor in 1974. He gained fame for living a simple life. Later, he served as mayor of the city of Oakland.

Brown, Edmund G. "Pat" (1905–1996) Politician. In 1962, Brown ran against Richard Nixon for governor of California and won. He helped develop the State Water Plan and the Master Plan for Education, which added three **campuses** to the University of California system.

Budge, Don (b. 1915) Professional athlete. In 1938, Budge was the first man to win the Grand Slam, the four biggest tournaments in tennis held in the same year. No one matched his accomplishment for 24 years.

Bunche, Ralph (1904–1971) Diplomat. The first African American to earn a Ph.D. from Harvard University, Bunche served in the United Nations. He helped work out the first peace agreement between Arabs and Israelis, and won the **Nobel Peace Prize** in 1950.

Nobel Peace Prize winner, Ralph Bunche

Cabrillo, Juan Rodríguez (?–1543) Explorer. Cabrillo explored California in 1542, while looking for a sea route between the Atlantic and Pacific Oceans. He was one of the first to sail both the San Diego Bay and Monterey Bay. He named the land *California*.

Silent film actor Charlie Chaplin

Chaplin, Charlie (1889–1997) Actor. Chaplin was the master movie comedian of his time. Classic films such as *City Lights* and *Modern Times* feature his character, "the little tramp." Chaplin helped found the United Artists movie studio.

Chávez, César (1927–1993) Labor leader. Chávez followed his heroes Martin Luther King Jr. and Mohandas Gandhi in seeking change through nonviolence. He founded the United Farm Workers (UFW) and developed the **boycott** to bring about change.

Clappe, Louise Smith (1819–1906) Writer. Clappe moved to the Sierra **foothills** during the gold rush. She wrote 23 famous letters to her sister as a character named "Dame Shirley." These letters were later published and are considered a classic account of California's gold rush days.

Coolbrith, Ina (1841–1928) Poet. At age ten, Coolbrith became the first white child to enter California, riding with James Beckwourth across the Beckwourth Pass in the Sierra Nevada. Later in life, she became the first public librarian of Oakland. She also wrote poetry and was named California's **poet laureate** in 1915.

Crespí, Juan (1721–1782) Explorer. This Spaniard traveled with some of the earliest explorers of California. He was part of a group that explored San Francisco Bay. His diaries are a record of the journeys.

Charles Crocker

Crocker, Charles (1822–1888) Businessperson. As one of the owners of the Central Pacific Railroad Company, Crocker helped build the **transcontinental** railroad. He managed the project, creating the largest workforce of employees California had ever seen. He also started Crocker Bank.

DeMille, Cecille Blount (1881–1959) Movie director. DeMille's movie *The Squaw Man* was America's first feature film. His greatest fame comes from films with huge casts of people, such as *The Ten Commandments.*

Disney, Walt (1901–1966) Movie producer. Disney arrived in Los Angeles in 1923 with $40 in his pocket. He created Mickey Mouse and Donald Duck, two of the world's most beloved cartoon characters. He also made *Snow White*, the first full-length animated feature movie. The Disney company is still giant in the entertainment business.

Entertainment giant Walt Disney

Eastwood, Clint (b. 1930) Actor. Eastwood created a new type of western hero in movies such as *The Good, the Bad, and the Ugly.* He often played a mysterious man of few words and no **loyalties.** Eastwood also served as mayor of the city of Carmel.

Frémont, John C. (1813–1890) Explorer, army officer, politician. Frémont came to California as a surveyor and soon became a national hero. He played a large role in conquering California in the Mexican-American War (1846–1848). He led **expeditions** to locate routes for the southern California railroad. In 1850, he became one of the first two California state senators.

Geisel, Theodor Seuss (1904-1991) Writer and illustrator. Best known as "Dr. Seuss," Geisel published nearly 50 books for children. His books combined humorous drawings with stories told with simple and nonsense words, and wild rhymes to entertain and educate children.

John C. Frémont

Hanks, Tom (b. 1956) Actor. Born in Concord, California, Tom Hanks has starred in movies such as *Saving Private Ryan, Big, Philadelphia,* and *Forrest Gump.* The last two films earned him two Academy Awards for best actor.

Hayakawa, S. I. (1906–1992) Philosopher and politician. Hayakawa made his name as an expert on semantics, which is the study of word meanings. As president of San Francisco State University, he gained fame for resisting the demands of student protesters. At the age of 70, he won a seat in the U.S. Senate.

Tom Hanks

Hearst, William Randolph (1863–1951) Publisher. Hearst built a chain of newspapers, starting with the *San Francisco Examiner.* His papers offered attention-grabbing headlines and entertainment rather than hard news. Hearst is best known today for his former home—a 160-room castle in San Simeon.

Herbert Hoover

Hoover, Herbert (1874–1964) President of the United States. Hoover graduated from Stanford University and oversaw construction of Hoover Dam, then the world's biggest dam. In 1928, he was elected the 32nd president of the United States. The Great **Depression** started in 1929, during his presidency, and Hoover was blamed for the problems it caused.

Ishi (ca. 1862–1916) Native Californian. Ishi was the last member of the Yahi Native American tribe. In 1911, he came out of hiding from the woods near Oroville. He lived with **anthropologist** Alfred Kroeber until his death. Kroeber's wife Theodora wrote a book about him called *Ishi: The Last of His Tribe.*

Jackson, Helen Hunt (1830–1885) Author. Jackson's book, *A Century of Dishonor,* tells how Native Americans were mistreated by the U.S. government. Her novel, *Ramona,* a romantic love story, was made into several movies.

Kearny, Stephen Watts (1794–1848) General. During the Mexican War, Kearny was ordered to conquer New

Ishi, the last Yahi tribe member

Photographer Dorothea Lange

Mexico and California. After gaining Santa Fe, he helped Stockton and Frémont control California, which they had already conquered. Kearny was then ordered to Mexico to become military commander of Veracruz. He died of yellow fever in 1848.

Kerouac, Jack (1922–1969) Writer. Kerouac developed an unstructured, flowing writing style that first made its appearance in *On the Road*, published in 1957. According to legend, Kerouac wrote this book in a single sitting without pausing or rewriting.

Lange, Dorothea (1895–1965) Photographer. Lange took pictures of people going through hard times. Her images make the viewer very sympathetic toward her subjects. Her best-known work includes pictures of people during the Great **Depression.**

Lawrence, Ernest Orlando (1901–1958) **Physicist.** Lawrence developed the cyclotron, a machine used for splitting atoms. His work led to the invention of the atomic bomb. Lawrence helped open the Lawrence Livermore Laboratory, in Livermore, California, which does important nuclear research.

London, Jack (1876–1916) Novelist. London wrote novels about working people as well as adventure stories set in the Alaska wilderness. His novel *Call of the Wild* is one of the most famous dog stories ever written.

Mason, Biddy (1818–1891) Pioneer. Born a slave in Mississippi, Mason was brought to California by her master. Slavery had been outlawed in California, so Mason sued for

Louis Mayer

her freedom and won. Late in life, she made a fortune in real estate, gave to charities, and started the first African-American church in Los Angeles.

Mayer, Louis (1885–1957) Movie producer. Mayer built Metro-Goldwyn-Mayer (MGM), created the movie studio system, and founded the Academy of Motion Pictures, which gives out the Academy Awards.

Montana, Joe (b. 1956) Football player. As quarterback of the San Francisco 49ers, Montana's talent led the 49ers to four Superbowls. He was the most valuable player in three of those games.

Morgan, Julia (1872–1957) **Architect.** The first woman architect in California, Morgan designed many buildings around the state. Her most famous creation is San Simeon, a 160-room castle she designed for William Randolph Hearst.

Muir, John (1838–1914) Naturalist. This Scottish-born wanderer loved the Sierra Nevada mountains, which he called "the range of light." He helped turn Yosemite Valley into a national park and founded the Sierra Club, a group that works to preserve places of great natural beauty.

Nixon, Richard Milhous (1913–1994) President of the United States. Nixon was elected the 37th president of the United States in 1968, and re-elected in 1972. In 1974, he was forced to resign from office because of a political scandal.

Richard Nixon

Oppenheimer, J. Robert (1904–1967) **Physicist.** Oppenheimer led the Manhattan Project, which developed the atomic bomb during World War II (1939–1945). In the 1950s, he was accused of disloyalty to the United States. No charges were ever proven, but Oppenheimer was denied access to any further information from the government.

General George S. Patton Jr.

Packard, David (1912–1996) **Engineer.** In 1938, working out of a Palo Alto garage, Packard and his partner William Hewlett founded one of the first high-tech companies. Hewlett-Packard grew into a giant in the computer **industry.**

Patton, George S. Jr. (1885–1945) General. Patton led the Allies' Third Army during World War II (1939–1945). This army took Berlin in 1945, and helped end World War II in Europe. Earlier, Patton had commanded U.S. forces in North Africa and Italy.

Pauling, Linus (1901–1994) Scientist. Pauling was the first man to win two individual Nobel Prizes. He won the Nobel Chemistry Prize in 1954. In 1962, he won the **Nobel Peace Prize** for his work against nuclear war. Pauling also tried to prove that Vitamin C could cure the common cold, but was unsuccessful.

Pico, Pío (1801–1894) Politician. Pico was the last Mexican governor of California. A revolutionary, Pico spent most of his time as governor struggling against

Pío Pico

rivals. When the Americans began their conquest of California, Pico fled to Mexico, and returned later as a private citizen.

Portolá, Gaspar de (ca. 1723–1786) Explorer. Portolá was the first governor of California appointed by Spain. He led the **expedition** that brought Father Junípero Serra to California in 1769. Leaving Serra in San Diego, Portolá continued north, and found San Francisco Bay.

Reagan, Ronald (b. 1911) President, actor. As the 40th president of the United States, Reagan's two terms stretched from 1981 to 1989. He started out as a movie actor. He served two terms as governor of California before becoming president. Reagan was known for lowering taxes, reducing welfare, and spending less money on education.

Ride, Sally K. (b. 1951) Astronaut. Born in Los Angeles, Ride was the first American woman in space. She served as communication officer on two space shuttles, *Columbia* and *Challenger.*

Salk, Jonas (1914–1995) Medical researcher. Salk developed the first polio **vaccine.** He later started the Salk Institute for Biological Studies in San Diego. His was the first

Astronaut Sally Ride

American team to identify the HIV virus, which causes AIDS. He spent the last years of his life researching an AIDS **vaccine.**

Saroyan, William (1908–1981) Writer. Saroyan wrote stories about Armenian-American life in the Central Valley. *The Time of Your Life* won the **Pulitzer Prize** in 1939.

Serra, Junípero (1713–1784) Missionary. This Franciscan **friar** founded **Mission** San Diego, which started the Spanish colonization of California. He founded several more missions, and he and his followers developed the agricultural economy of California.

Sinclair, Upton (1878–1968) Writer, crusader. Sinclair saw much wrong in the world, and he tried to fix it. He did this first by writing novels, then by running for governor of California. After a tough race, he was not elected.

Upton Sinclair

Stanford, Leland (1824–1893) Businessperson. Stanford helped start the Central Pacific company, which built the western half of the **transcontinental** railroad. Stanford co-founded the state's Republican Party, served as the state's first Republican governor, and then went to Washington, D.C., as its senator. He also founded Stanford University.

John Steinbeck

Steinbeck, John (1902–1968) Writer. Steinbeck won the Nobel Prize for literature in 1962. His best-known novel, *The Grapes of Wrath*, tells the story of an Oklahoma family that moved to California during the Great

Depression. Some of his other novels are set in Salinas, his hometown.

Levi Strauss

Stockton, Robert (1795–1866) Naval officer. Admiral Stockton commanded the fleet that sailed to California in 1846. He then gathered an army and started the conquest of California from the Mexicans.

Strauss, Levi (1830–1902) Businessperson. During the gold rush, Strauss made pants that were strong enough to hold up through the work the miners were doing. Later, these were called "blue jeans." Strauss's company became the biggest clothing manufacturer in the world.

Temple, Shirley (b. 1928) Actress, diplomat. Probably the biggest child star of all time, Temple began her movie career at age three. By age ten, she had the seventh highest income in the United States. She left the movie **industry** as a teenager and later served as U.S. ambassador to Ghana under her married name, Shirley Temple Black.

Mariano Vallejo

Vallejo, Mariano Guadalupe (1808–1890) Political leader. Vallejo was born in California, and served as the military commander of northern California in the last days of Mexican rule. He founded the town of Sonora, favored the American takeover of California, encouraged his daughters to marry "Yankees," and gave land to settlers from the United States. After California became a state, the new government took away most of his land.

Warren, Earl (1891–1974) Politician, judge. A three-time governor of California, Warren was appointed Chief Justice of the U.S. Supreme Court in 1953. He served for sixteen years. In his most famous decision, the court outlawed **segregation** in schools. His court also worked to strengthen the Bill of Rights.

Wayne, John (1907–1979) Actor. Born Marion Morrison, Wayne started his movie career by doing stunts, but he soon changed his name and switched to acting. Playing a **rugged** Western hero, he became the most famous movie cowboy of all time.

Venus (left) and Serena Williams

Williams, Venus and Serena (b. 1980 and 1981) Professional athletes. Venus and Serena Williams have been playing tennis since age six. With their father as their coach, the sisters have won many tournaments, as well as Olympic gold medals in the 2000 Summer Olympic Games. As of 2002, they have thirteen grand slam titles between them, three of which they earned while playing as partners.

Woods, Eldrick (Tiger) (b. 1975) Professional athlete. Nicknamed "Tiger" after a Vietnamese soldier who was a friend of his father's in Vietnam, Woods is well-known in the sports world. Born in Cypress, California, Tiger has been playing golf all his life. He was featured in *Golf Digest* at age five, having already attracted attention for his golf skills. In 2002, Tiger won his third Masters tournament, becoming the youngest player ever to win seven Professional Golfers' Association (PGA) major tournaments.

Map of California

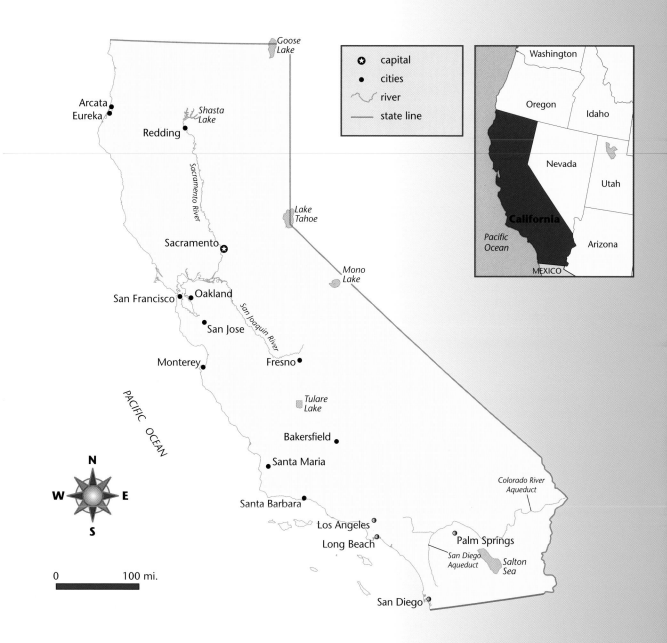

Legend:
- ✪ capital
- • cities
- ~ river
- — state line

Goose Lake

Arcata
Eureka
Shasta Lake
Redding

Sacramento River

Lake Tahoe

Sacramento ✪

Mono Lake

San Francisco
Oakland
San Jose
San Joaquin River

Monterey
Fresno

Tulare Lake

Bakersfield
Santa Maria

Santa Barbara
Colorado River Aqueduct
Los Angeles
Long Beach
Palm Springs
San Diego Aqueduct
Salton Sea
San Diego

PACIFIC OCEAN

N
W   E
S

0   100 mi.

Inset map:
Washington
Oregon
Idaho
Nevada
Utah
California
Pacific Ocean
Arizona
MEXICO

Glossary

adobe heavy clay used to make sun-dried bricks

ancestry line of people from which a person descends

anthropologist one who studies human culture

architect person who designs buildings

boycott to refuse to have dealings with someone or buy a certain product until a demand is met

campus grounds of a university or other school

Catholic Church original church of Christianity centered in Rome, Italy. Members of the Catholic Church are called **Catholics.**

census government count of population and the gathering of information about that population

Christianity believing in the teachings of Jesus

culture customs, beliefs, tools, and overall way of life of a group

custom something a person or group does that has been done for a long time and has become a habit

delicatessen store that sells prepared foods such as meats, cheeses, and preserves

depression time when business in general is doing poorly

descend born of; come from a given source

discrimination unfair treatment of people based on their differences from others

diverse having variety

engineer person who specializes in mechanical devices

entrepreneur someone who takes advantage of a new type of business opportunity

ethnic belonging to a group with a particular culture

expedition organized journey of a group of people

famine time when food is scarce and people are starving

fast to go without food for a cause or purpose

foothill low hill at the base of a mountain or mountain range

friar member of a Christian brotherhood that has accepted poverty as a way of life

immigration act of moving to another country to settle. A person who immigrates is an **immigrant.**

industry group of businesses that offer a similar product or service

inland not near the sea coast

Islam religion based on the life and teachings of Mohammed

Latino person from a Latin American country who speaks Spanish; the term *Hispanic* is also sometimes used to describe such a person

legacy something handed down from one's ancestors

lieutenant governor second-in-command of a state, after the governor

loyalty   faithfulness to one's country or group

migrant farm worker   farm laborer from another country who comes to work in the United States during a growing season

minority   person who is different in some way from most people in a group

mission   group that sets forth on a task, particularly to spread certain religious views

monk   male member of a religious community

Nobel Peace Prize   award given each year to someone who has promoted peace

order   organized religious group, often of monks or nuns

physicist   specialist in physics

poet laureate   official poet of a state or country

prejudice   unfair judgment formed before any facts are examined

Pulitzer Prize   award given in the United States in several fields, including writing

refugee   person who flees from a war or other danger in his or her country

relocating   moving to another place

revolt   go against the rule of a ruler or the government

riot   outbreak of wild violence on the part of a crowd

rugged   robust or sturdy

segregation   setting one type of people apart from others

squatter   one who unlawfully lives on land he or she doesn't own

strike   group decision to stop working until certain demands are met

tactic   means used to gain a certain end in a competition

transcontinental   extending across a continent

treason   crime of trying to overthrow a government

union   organization of workers to help them get better working conditions

vaccine   material used to protect against disease

war-torn   condition of a land in which war is raging

More Books to Read

Harder, Dan. *A Child's California*. Portland: WestWinds Press, 2000.

Kennedy, Teresa. *California*. Danbury, Conn.: Children's Press, 2001.

Pelta, Kathy. *California*. Minneapolis: Lerner Publications Company, 2001.

St. Antione, Sara, ed. *Stories from Where We Live—The California Coast*. Minneapolis: Milkweed Editions, 2001.

Index

About the Author

Tamim Ansary lives in San Francisco, California. He has worked for twenty years as a textbook editor and writer. His nonfiction series for children include *Holiday Histories* and *Native Americans.* Currently, he writes a learning column for Encarta Online.